OUR STARS

Written and Illustrated by

ANNE ROCKWELL

SCHOLASTIC INC.

New York Toronto London Auckland Sydney
Mexico City New Delhi Hong Kong

When night comes,
I can see billions of stars
twinkling in the dark sky.

The sun that shines in the daytime
and keeps us warm is really a star.

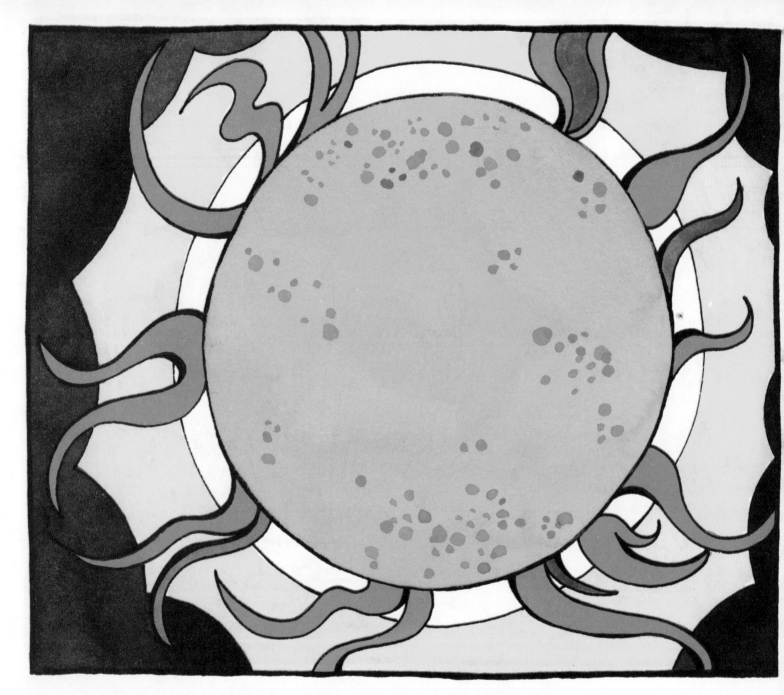

A star is made of fiery gas.
It gives off brilliant light.

Some stars are so far away
that their fire has burned out
by the time the brightness reaches us.

Long ago, people imagined pictures
in groups of stars and gave them names.
These are called constellations.

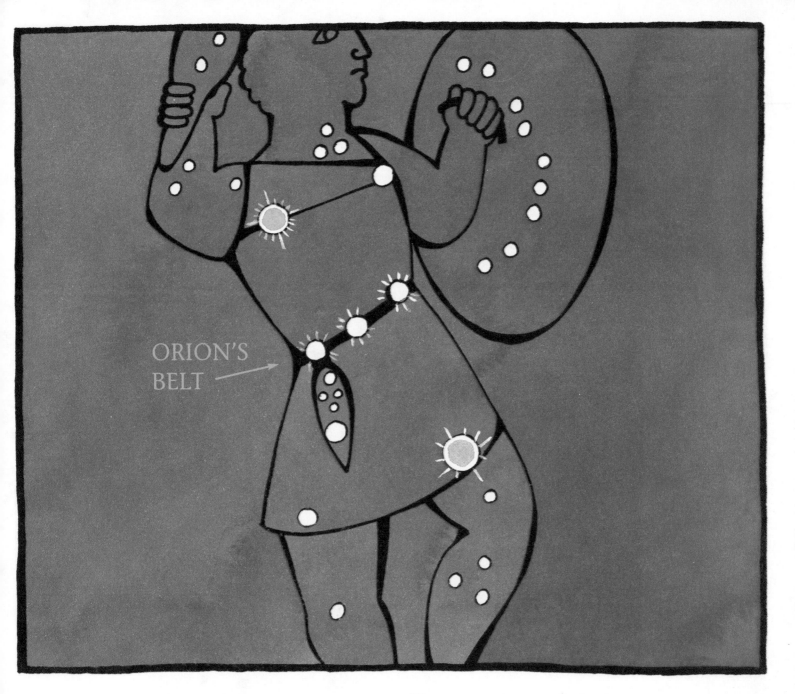

ORION'S
BELT

Constellations can tell us many things.
When we see Orion the Hunter in the sky,
we know it is the season to harvest what we planted.

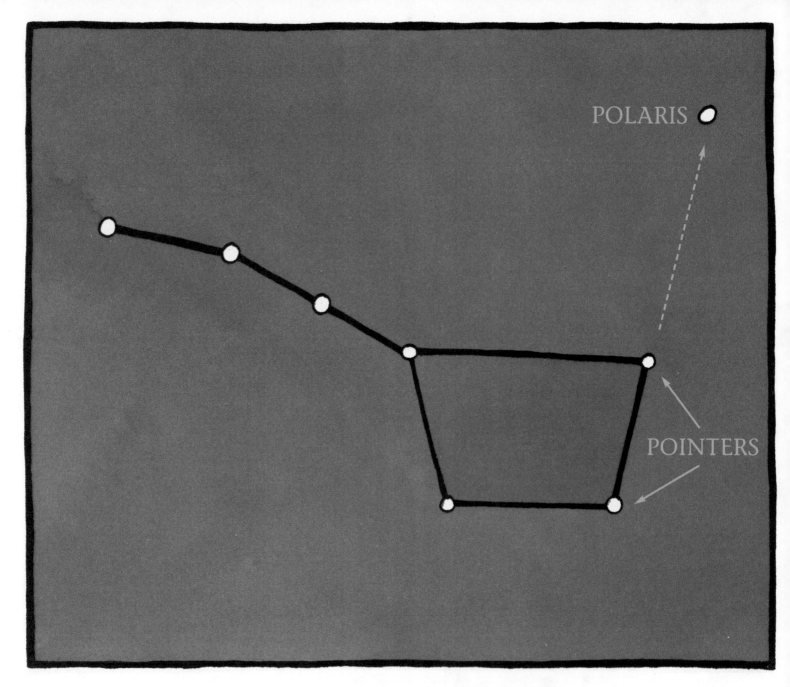

All year long, the Big Dipper points
toward a star named Polaris.
Polaris is also called the North Star.

We always see Polaris in the northern sky.
If you know which way north is,
you can always find your way in the darkness.

Sometimes before the stars come out,
we can see a bright light
dangling low on the horizon.

It looks like a star, but it isn't.
It is the planet Venus.
Stars twinkle, but planets glow with steady light.

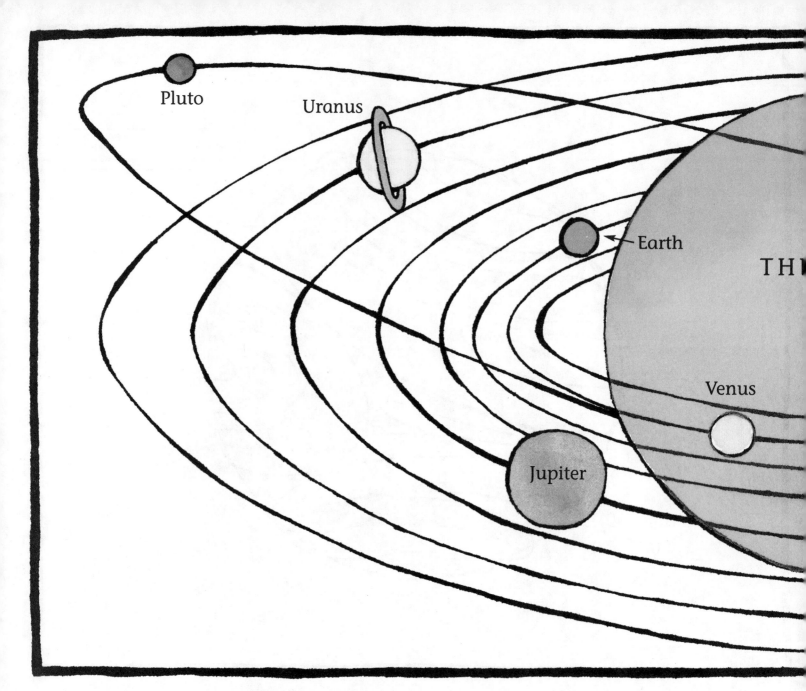

When something in space goes around something else,
it is in orbit. Planets orbit around stars.
Planets get their light from the star that shines on them.

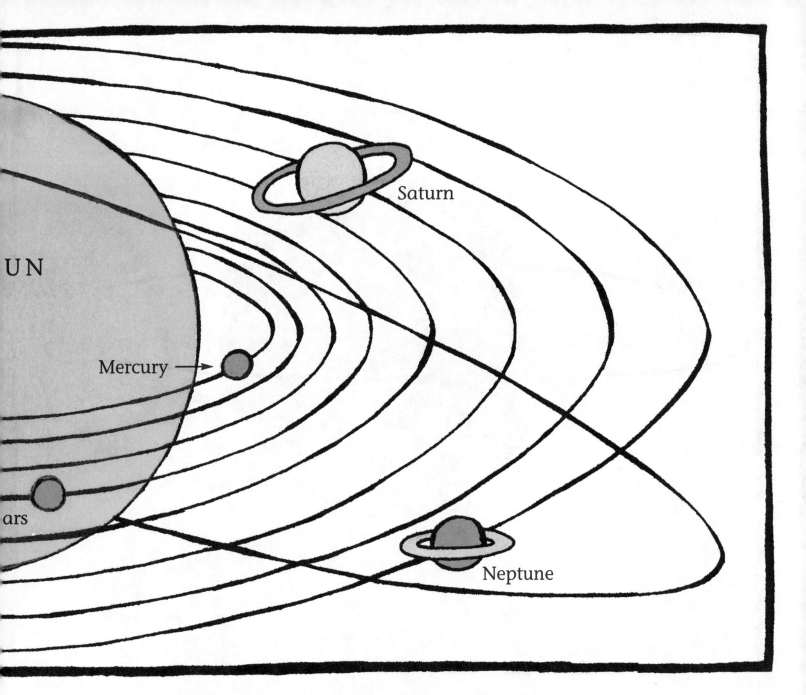

Earth where we live is a planet.
Earth orbits around the sun.
The sun and its planets make up our solar system.

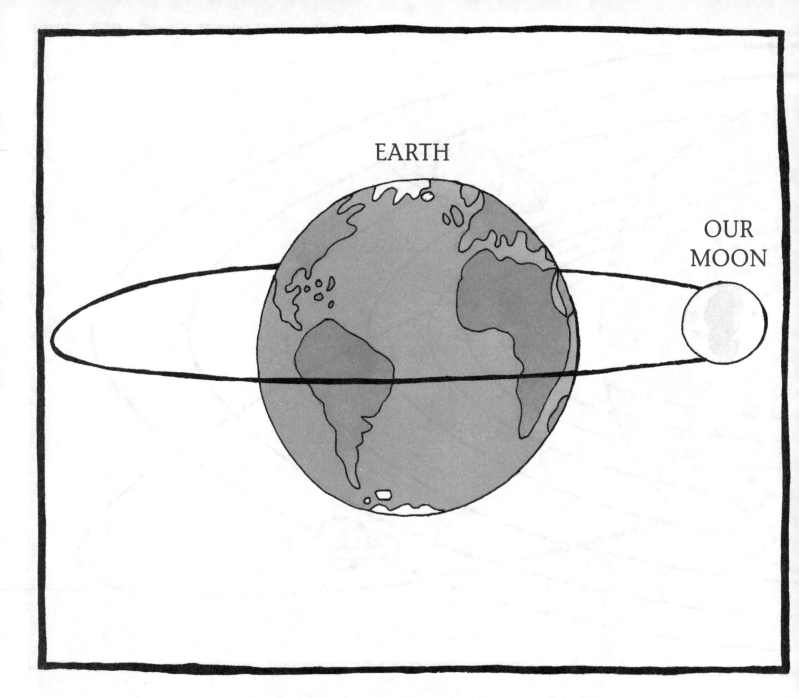

Moons orbit around planets.
Some planets have many moons.
Earth has just one.

Our moon seems to change its shape each night,
but it doesn't. It is always round.
We just can't see all of it.

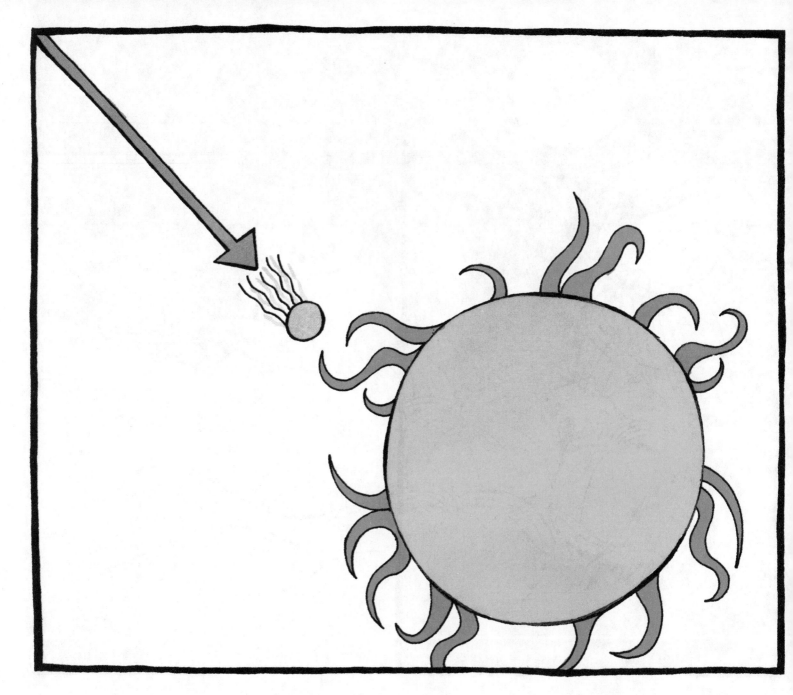

At the outer edge of our solar system
there are big chunks of ice.
We can't see them until they orbit close to the sun.

Then the ice starts to melt
and forms a long, bright tail.
This chunk of ice with a shining tail is a comet.

Streaks of light that look like faraway fireworks
are meteors. We call them shooting stars.

When meteors zoom close to Earth,
they usually burn up in the air.
Sometimes one falls and makes a crater in the ground.

Stars, planets, comets, and meteors
are all part of the universe.
People have always wanted to know about our universe.

That's why we study stars through giant telescopes.
That's why we send satellites into space.
But the universe is much greater than we can measure.

Astronauts have gone to the moon,
but no one has ever gone to any star.
I think our universe will always be a mystery.

We'll go on looking at our beautiful stars each night—
looking and wondering.

For Juliann Joy

ISBN 0-439-16580-6

Copyright © 1999 by Anne Rockwell.
All rights reserved.
Published by Scholastic Inc., 555 Broadway, New York, NY 10012,
by arrangement with Harcourt Brace & Company.
SCHOLASTIC and associated logos are trademarks
and/or registered trademarks of Scholastic Inc.

13 12 11 10 9 8 7 6   4 5 6 7 8/0

Printed in the U.S.A.   40

First Scholastic printing, October 1999

The illustrations in this book were done in gouache and silkscreen.
The display type was set in Schwere.
The text type was set in Stone Informal.
Designed by Linda Lockowitz